POEMS OF RYME FOR A HAPPY TIME

BY

RICO LAGATTUTA

Library of Congress Control Number: 2024908113

SHARE WITH YOUR FAMILY

SHARE WITH YOUR FRIENDS

READ ALONE

YOU WILL SMILE

THEY WILL SMILE

BECAUSE

ALL IS GOOD!

TABLE OF CONTENT

GOODBYE MY FRIEND

(Yesterday I lost a friend, a friend from our early start to our too early end).

Last night, I looked up to the sky
    and saw what looked like a light go by.
It did not linger, it did not stay,
    but as it went it flickered my way.
I thought to myself, was that flicker just for me
    or was that flicker for all to see?

I went to bed
    and hard I did try
To clear my head
    of that flicker in the sky.

Then low and behold,
    it dawned on me,
Of just what that flicker
    had to be.

My friend saying his last goodbye.
    I did not tear. I did not cry.
But as he passed, I did see
    his very last wave from that heavenly sea.

Rest in peace my friend.

TIME PAST

O lament I,
Where have they gone?
Spent, spent, neither right nor wrong!

Return, return
Come back to me!
Gone, gone how can this be?

I seek, I search
To mend my ways
For long do I for the good old days!

LOST CHILDHOOD

Where have all the children gone?
I cannot find my friends.

When we grew up our childhood left
Our friendships all did end.

Where have all the children gone?
The bonds with friends did end.

Do we discard our trust and love,
Because our childhood ends?

JOURNEY'S END

There was a man from London town
    from London town came he.
He came to see his maiden fair
    from far off land came he.

He traveled neigh on twenty days
    he rode from dawn to dusk.
And when he reached his journeys end
    he found her gone and lost.

He searched the land for many years
    o'er hill and dale and plain.
Too old to live too tired to search
    to death his body lain.

He found his love in far off land,
    and now the story goes
They live and romp all through the clouds
    these two happy souls. These two happy souls.

A NEW NIGHT'S PRAYER

Now I lay me down to sleep
And thank the Lord for the soul I keep.

And tomorrow, when I awake
It is for the love I give and the love I take.

God bless everyone in the whole wide world!

BE YOU

You have got to be honest
You have got to be true
To family and friends
You have got to be you!

Stand up to bullies.
And the bad guys too
You must be courageous.
You have got to be you.

I SEE WHAT I SEE

The dew in the grass reminded me
Of a bird I once saw up in a tree.

How you may ask do you see
From the dew in the grass
A bird up a tree?

Not in the grass do I see
A bird in the grass
Up in the tree

Just the dew in the grass do I see
Reminding me of a bird in a tree.

I MUST BE BLIND

I must be blind
  for I cannot see
The gift the Lord
  bequeath to me.

Why not a star
  that shines on high
Or a drama man
  so the ladies cry?

A numbers man
  who sees the end
Or a master of chess
  or of lesser men.

A teacher of students
  so they will enhance
The knowledge I give them
  so their lot will advance.

A man of thought
  a thinker I'd be
So people will yearn
  to be like me.

Perhaps an artist
    with a special flair
Idolized by all
    who just stand and stare.
A judge, a lawyer
    or some type of chief
So all would come
    for some sought relief.

The field I'm in
    I not toil with hand
But no great office
    do I command!

There must be something
    I cannot see
That the Lord
    did give to me.

He gave to so many
    and not just to some
So why must it be I
    on the bottom rung?

I must be blind
    for I cannot see
The gift the Lord
    bequeath to me!

WHAT GOES UP MUST COME DOWN

Step by step
    he climbed up high
Til on the floor
    he had to lie.

The task was great
    but conqueror be he
Til the very top wrung
    did touch his knee.

Once on top
    it was clear to all
That down he'd flop.
    he was destined to fall.

And thus it ended
    with a slam
And gaze they did
    upon falling man.

This poem may seem
    a little crass
But that could be you
    flat on your ass.

LEARNING AND WISDOM

Ode to the people
Who know too well
Opinions that differ
In hearts do dwell

From whence they came
They cannot tell
But therein they lie
Til heaven or hell.

What brought them forth, they cannot say,
Perhaps a thought that's gone astray.
Or maybe a wish
Long not filled
Perhaps just a dream lay unfulfilled.

Acceptance is
A virtue of life
Rejection causes
Naught but strife.

Learning and wisdom
Escape their lot
For knowledge is born
When shackles rot.

Acquiescence of life
I do not accept.
Nor a profound wisdom
Do I reject.

If my way your way
Becomes the issue
Then problem 's end
Will always miss you.

INDEPENDENCY

Cast off their irons of restraint!
Spoon feed them the value of independency.

Like the farmer, plant your seed!
Like the mustard seed, watch it grow.

Untie their bonds of dependency!
Restore their freedom and dignity.

A helping hand is a gift from a friend.
But handouts are binds, to a master, without end.

EXPRESSION

The beauty of man is the outward expression
    of his innermost feelings.
Pity not the man whose feelings are not chaste
    for his is the beauty, not in the expression but
of being expressed.

Glorify the tarnished and the stained
    though their expression is colored by their
sordid individualism
    Praise their ignoble self
for they are expressed.

    Shed more than tears of apathy for he
who has gorged himself with loneliness.
    The lonely are the ugly
their world is a void, encased in a shell of
nothingness.

PASSIONLESS

I see lights against the black canvas.
        They shine not bright nor dim.
But glow they do - all brothers
        against the black canvas.

Some see romance as they gaze on high
        others dream dreams, while lovers sigh.
Some see adventure, upon the ship of thrust
        trying to satisfy their nagging lust.

Children wonder star on high
        how do you twinkle in the sky?
For some you twinkle a very bright light
        you twinkle by day, you twinkle by night,
twinkling them an imagination bright.

        I see lights against a black canvas.
No bright lights!
        No dim lights!
Just a black canvas with lights.

I AM WHAT I AM

As a rock I sit
    upon my convictions.
But not immobile
    when faced with restrictions.

Like a tree, I've learned to sway
    when a gentle breeze comes my way.
Or fall I would upon my knees
    if a strong wind came instead of a breeze.

Like the wind
    gentle or strong
I can wrong the right,
    I can right the wrong.

I have a mind
    I voice my thoughts
But mask my words
    and clothe my faults.

I labor for laws
    a taker of gold
I am scorned , I am loved
    by the young and the old.

I stand as a witness
    of things yet to be
But cower with allies
    of issues at sea.

I'm a leader bred by wisdom
    a student of life
My rights and my wrongs
    are cradled in strife.

I know where I've been
    understand where I am
As for tomorrow
    there is no plan.

I'll know when I get there
    I'll have made a decision
For as you surmise
    I'm a politician.

ILLUMINATION

I came upon a clearing
I saw a wondrous sight
An array of high tall buildings
Aglow in luminous light.

I wandered about blindly
Then it came to me
The lights of which I gazed upon
Were reflections of what could be.

Now with eyes wide open
And a mind not filled with doubt
I saw structures in the clearing
As they mingled all about.

The habitants in the clearing
Did not linger there
They were entrance and they were dreaming
As they mingled without care.

For in a world filled with light
You can finally see
What your life could be like
And who you could truly be.

So pursue they did
And dreams do come true
For in this wondrous clearing
Life belongs to you.

Once inside the clearing
With eyes open so I could to see
All things I have ever dreamt
Were now possible for me.

No longer cloaked in darkness
No longer scourged by doubt
I pursue the dreams I've always dreamt
And seek my way about.

To forge on through the darkness
Is a dreamer's right
And all the dreams I've ever dreamt
Are now reachable in sight.

Now I walk amongst tall buildings
Aglow in luminous light
For I came upon a clearing
And there I saw the light!

THE SEASONS OF LIFE

The snow does fall and it does drift
and with this weather I have a riff.
These old bones say, “I am cold.”
“Yes” I say, “because you're old.”

The winter did crest and I did my best
to try to keep warm and weather the storm.
I lost the battle.   My teeth do rattle.
My fingers and toes, yes, they are old. And my
fingers and toes are very cold.

“Where are you old sun your warmth do I pray
to visit with me on this cold cold day.”
“I did visit you some, but you paid me no heed
for it was just for yourself you only had need.”

From summer to fall to winter to spring
it’s life to earth it’s a beautiful thing!
In spring I did nourish. In summer I did flourish.
And in the fall, I did thrive for the reach of my
drive.

Now winter is here
and now a new fear!
Spring is gone and summer just flew,
and fall is a memory failing me too.

Now winter is all that I have left
except for the memories of what I liked best.
But winter too will soon just end
completing the seasons of life's journey end.

BOWLS

This morning my breakfast bowl was empty! Yesterday my breakfast bowl was empty.

A man came to my door. "Follow me," he said. "Lend me your support and there will be something in your breakfast bowl."

If I do not follow, tomorrow my breakfast bowl will be empty. If I follow and lend my support, tomorrow my breakfast bowl may be empty. Tomorrow, my breakfast bowl may not be empty. I woke up this morning my breakfast bowl was empty.

I woke up this morning my life bowl was empty. Yesterday my life bowl was empty. As for tomorrow I am not sure. If I follow and lend my support my life bowl may be filled with hope. I follow.

I woke up this morning my life bowl was not empty. My life bowl was not just full. My life bowl overflowed with hope. My breakfast bowl was full.

I woke up this morning my dependence bowl was full. My breakfast bowl was not empty. My hope bowl was empty! Tomorrow, my breakfast bowl will not be empty. My hope bowl will be empty.

My dependence bowl will overflow. "Follow me," he said, "and your breakfast bowl will not be empty." I followed. Now I am empty!

I hunger not for food. I hunger not for dependence. I hunger for hope. I wait for a new man to come to my door.

THE GIFTEE

(from Bullies' East men's john wall. Author unknown)

The Giftee gives us the gift to see ourselves
as others see us.

Who are we to say that others see us as giants
as we see ourselves instead of elves.

What are we but interpretations
of our own perfections?

THE FUTURE

What is in the future?
No one really knows.
To forge into the future
You need not be brave, nor bold.

For the future comes to visit
Every moment of every day
No placard or sign on the door
Can make it go away.

So what is in the future?
An adventure I am told.
Not for just the brave of heart
Not for just the bold.

You don't have to invite him in
Or encourage him to stay.
He is what he is, a persistent sort
And just won't go away.

Embrace him with open arms
And smile as you pass the day.
For the longer you enjoy the visit
The longer he will stay.

JUST ASKING

Why is it that the grass is greener
From the spot on which I stand
No matter how I tend the garden
Mine never looks grand?

Why is it that my neighbor's flowers
Grow so big and tall
And every one that I grow
Grows so doggone small?

Why is it that the food I cook
With patience in my home
Never tastes quite as good
When I eat alone?

Why is it that the phone does ring
When I'm wrapped in fascination
Just at that explicit time
Interrupting my concentration?

Why is it that each day I do
Not the things I planned
Yet fill my time with things to do
And end up in a jam?

Why is it that I ask of thee,
To help me understand
When way down deep in my heart of hearts
I just don't give a damn?

NO NEED TO EXPLAIN

She understood not my poem
    and expressed without reservation
her total lack of like for it
    and her unreserved indignation.

I pondered to explain it
    but thought the better of
reread what I had written
    guided from above.

The poem was very clear to me
    the message contained therein
exploited the given premise
    of mankind filled with sin.

The message very pointed
    did not exacerbate
but pointed out every vice of man
    spared need to elaborate.

The problem with this poem I found
    was what it contained therein
a message not to her liking
    was my major sin.

All poems are written from the mind
       and poets do profess
that poems of love for the heart
       with readers they do best.

But poems can be so many things
       for this one I'm invoking
that this particular poem of mine
       was penned for thought provoking.

FREEDOMS

Fear not my son.
You are as safe as safe can be.
For You were born
In the land of the free.

Oh my mother, how can this be?
There is no one safe in the land of the free.
My money they take at their request
As for the taxes I pay, I'm taxed like the rest.

My freedom is gone,
So, I must comply
To the dictates of those who rule.
But why?

The air that I breathe
I'm told it is free
But it's the air that the government
Gives to me.

The school that I went to
Just to learn
Now cost a fortune
From the money I earn.

The media tells me
What they want me to hear.
And they void all the laws
That we once held dear.

Freedom of speech
Has long become dead
Lest I speak the words
That I do dread.

It's a crime they say
If I break a law
But it's the laws they make
That make me fall.

For the laws that I like they will not keep,
They make me obey the ones that will reap
Order for them and not for me
So tell me my mother how am I free?

SLOWLY

(A Line Too Long)

Here I stand, not on desolate spot,
Waiting my turn to use the pot.

Thoughts are flowing from my mind,
As I wait my turn and bide my time.
And conjure up all restrain.
As I stand my place in physical pain.

The sounds I hear are of levers pressed
And water flushed down plumbed egress.
And with each one a brand-new fear
Of not reaching the fixture as I draw near.

But why before me, must each one stall,
Before the fixture on the wall
Long enough to make me strain
And forced to endure this most physical pain?

“Hurry up” is my big plea
“For I really do have to pee!”

But the line is long so I must wait
And pray to God to hold the gate
And not let the flow of nature’s call
Embarrass me before them all.

So here I stand, not on desolate spot,
Waiting my turn to use the pot.
New thoughts are raging in my head
As I wait my turn to forge ahead.

“Hurry, hurry,” I want to yell.
“I've got to go can't you tell?”
The line is moving oh so slow,
“Hurry, hurry, I've got to go.”

Yet in silence do I stand muscles controlled by demand.
For fear of embarrassment, I do not speak
Concerned that more than words would leak,
Right here on this spot and expose the world to my human lot.

Now louder sounds of levers pressed
and water flowing through plumbed egress.
And with each pressed sound I hear
To porcelain fixture I draw near-slowly!

JACKASS HILL

Born in the village of Pleasanton
In the forest of serene bliss,
The smiling child longs to please
And is pleased by a heart warm kiss.

Off in the distance stands a hill
The child must someday climb.
Destined is this child of God
To leave the womb behind.

The grade is slow, and the child does nestle
Amid the shade of trees.
But climb he must and climb he will
At first a few degrees.

A refreshing pause at four or five,
From turbulent years, at last
Confused were we of twos and threes
But those terrible years did pass.

The teenage years have come of age,
And now time sets the stage.
For each and every one of them
Has passage through this faze.

So up they climb, “Please reach the top”
Is every parent's prayer.
But question them their climbing skills
Only strong ones choose to dare.

The slope is steep, but all must pass
This challenge of their years.
And while they climb they paused to rest
While parents forge their tears.

With peers aplenty, they dawdle and wade
And pace their climb too slow.
At least to all the parents there
Who wish it were not so.

Then they reach that magic age
For each one it is true
Up, on and at the top
Cause through the years they grew.

The hill’s been there since time began
And each has had to climb,
Till up, over, and once on top
They leave the climb behind.

But climb they did and so did we
And so must all of them.
For years to come each child must climb
And climb until the end.

Once on top, they see so clear what foliage blocked from view.
Yet watch we must our children climb and wish that they but knew,
That to be on top, without the climb, would tarnish all the thrill
Of standing there and looking down from atop of Jackass Hill.

Made in the USA
Coppell, TX
03 September 2024

36561251R00024